EARN EASY MONEY IN ONE DAY

How Anyone Can Boost Income with Quick Treasure Hacks, Simple Cash Gigs And Legit Side Hustles Without Spending Any Money

Tina Kay

Copyright © 2024 by Native Sun Publishing LLC

All rights reserved.

No portion of this book may be reproduced, or stored in a retrieval system, or transmitted in any form or by any mean, electronic, mechanical, photocopying, recording, or otherwise, without express written permission of the publisher or author, except as permitted by U.S. copyright law.

ISBN-13: 9798303122642

ISBN-10: 1477123456

Cover design by: T.Kay – Canva

Library of Congress Control Number: 2018675309

Printed in the United States of America

For My Mom

Contents

1. INTRODUCTION — 1
2. EASY, QUICK MONEY HACKS — 4
3. LET'S MAKE MONEY — 11
4. HIDDEN SPENDING — 17
5. WORK FROM HOME — 21
6. CASH GIGS & SIDE HUSTLES 101 — 24
7. ONLINE QUICK CASH GIGS — 28
8. LEGITIMATE SIDE HUSTLES — 32
9. SCAM AND TAX IMPLICATIONS — 34
10. CONCLUSION — 36
11. RESOURCES — 38

CHAPTER 1

INTRODUCTION

WELCOME TO MY LITTLE book about earning money easily and quickly without spending a dime. I had so much fun writing it because my journey, as the author, took me down memory lane with gratitude and joy.

My primary objective is that the following information is useful and will aid anyone in making money today. You already know, have heard of and or read about most of these ideas. There are no new revelations. This book has no "get rich quick" schemes, claims, or programs in this book. I have merely organized, within these chapters, what we already know with regards to making additional revenue in the fastest way possible. I hope to enlighten anyone reading it of simple, tried and true enterprising hacks as well as credible opportunities. I have researched cash gigs and side hustles both of which can provide anyone with additional income. I focused on the ones that are easy to do and get you paid quickly.

I grew up in a small town in Idaho. My friends and I knew how to work and earn money as a kid. It was a necessity. In my family, we had everything we needed growing up, but there was no extra money for our wants. My parents were practical and ensured we understood the value of money and how to earn it. As the oldest of seven children in a blended family, an extra dollar was true wealth to my siblings and me. I knew exactly how to make a dollar in an hour or less.

I do have this fond memory of making fast cash as a child. It was summer, and I was 11 years old. Two of my friends and I started our club. We were organized and serious about this club; we wore matching, hand-painted t-shirts. We devised a money-making plan to buy a big bag of potato chips for our meeting. We needed $2 for the snack. We went to the next-door neighbor, introduced ourselves, and asked for an egg for our club. After her initial bewilderment and a few giggles, she gave us one egg. I'm sure the matching T-shirts helped. We took the egg and went across the street to the next neighbor. We used the same introduction and explained we were fundraising for our club. We asked if she wanted to buy the egg. Again, with similar bemusement, that lady gave us five cents for the egg. Ah, our strategy was working. We then went to the next house and asked for an egg, which we did get. Then, we sold that egg at the following home and got 10 cents. We had earned fifteen cents within a few minutes and were thrilled. We continued this little venture down the street. It wasn't but an hour, and we had our two dollars. With no money, we earned enough for a big bag of potato chips and an orange soda that we all shared. Success. Ladybugs Karen P. and Julie B., I thank you.

In high school, my classmates and I took fundraising to a new level for our "Senior Sneak" class trip. We only had four years to earn it because, as freshmen, we set our sights on traveling from Idaho to Disneyland and Universal Studios in California. We found so many good ways of earning that money. Our best money-making venture was selling baked potatoes at the football games each of our four years. Some were eaten, but most were purchased for hand warmers while sitting in those cold, snowy bleachers. I thank the farmers who donated the potatoes, our Moms who wrapped them in foil and baked them, and our Dads who hauled them to the football games in coolers. We did indeed take that trip. About 25 of us, more than half my class, and our chaperons share those once-in-a-lifetime memories, but we all earned the funds to get there. Love you, WHS Class of '81.

The 2008 financial crisis caused the city I worked for to file for bankruptcy. As a result employee pay was cut from 20% and higher for anyone who stayed working for the city. I stayed, but this unexpected and difficult circumstance fueled my interest in finding ways to diversify my income to be better prepared for the life's next challenge. I understand the value and benefits of multiple income streams and have been inspired by all the creative ways people make money in the world today.

Please continue reading, as I will share a few 21st-century money-making ventures anyone can do easily, quickly, and for free.

Chapter 2

EASY, QUICK MONEY HACKS

THE DAYS OF WALKING door to door and asking for an egg and then selling it are long gone. But, read on for an instant way to get money.

Remember the days when all you needed was a bit of change? You may need to feed a parking meter, buy a newspaper from a machine, or purchase something from a vending machine. We all carried change in our pockets more often than not. That change would often end up outside of our pockets. These are the places I always found change:

- The couch and chair cushions

- The pockets of pants and jackets

- The bottom of the washer drum

- The dryer lint trap

- The laundry room floor

- A vehicle console, glove-box, and in and under the

seats

- The junk drawer
- An old piggy bank

Try finding change in these locations at your home or office. More often than not, anyone will see change in minutes, especially if they live with a large family or have numerous visitors in their home and vehicle. This was a typical hack in college, too, for when you just needed a few coins for the vending machine. This was a game for my nieces and nephews at my house when they were young. If they found money on the floor it was theirs to keep. I always got a kick out of them rushing off and scrambling around looking for treasure immediately after our greeting hugs were done.

Finders keepers? I will caution you to ask if you are allowed to keep what you find. Also, the money you find in clothing belongs to the owner of those garments.

To prove my point, I just found this treasure under the couch cushion and in the car console. Oh, I see I need to do some vacuuming, eeew.

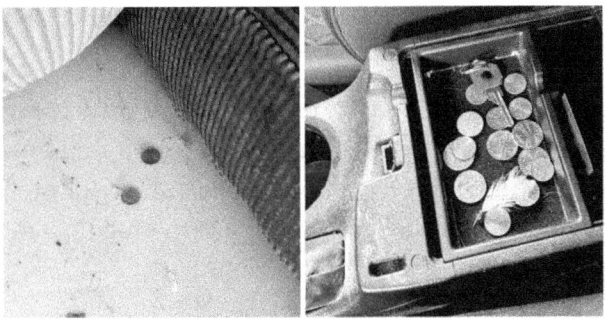

Under couch cushion and the car console.

I realize the younger generations do not carry change around. Our culture has evolved into using credit cards and cell phone apps to make purchases, including those at vending machines. But a few of us 'old school' types still have change jingling in our pockets and saved in a piggy bank or jar.

The Piggy Bank or Change Jar - Maybe you or someone you know collects change. My dad has been saving his change for as long as I can remember. He would separate the denominations into their separate containers. Once they were full, he would head to the bank and cash them in. He was good at guessing how much was in each one, too. I went with him one time to cash in. He got over $150. He did this at 82 years old, and I also do it.

My change jar and an old-fashion piggy bank for comparison.

I took the jar to my local grocery store, where there was a self-serve Coinstar change machine. I drove from home to the store and then completely poured the contents of my jar into the machine. I took the receipt to the cashier, who handed me the $164.40. It only took me 37 minutes.

All that change really adds up!

Scratchers and Lottery Tickets - You've scratched and meticulously checked them; behold, they are winners. Do you have them sitting in a stack on your desk or table? I've seen these little collections many times. That is cash just sitting right there. Turn those tickets in and get that dinero.

Return a Recent Purchase - Buyer's remorse is genuine. If you still have the receipt and have not used it, return it and get your money back. If you don't have a receipt, some businesses will credit the purchase price back to the credit card with which it was purchased.

Recycle Cans and Bottles - In California, you pay a California Redemption Value (CRV) fee when you buy a beverage in a can or bottle. You get that money back when you take your empty containers to a recycling center. The state designed this plan to encourage us to recycle those containers. You earn five cents for sizes under 24 ounces and 10 cents for containers 24 ounces or larger. Milk, wine, and distilled spirits are not CRV recyclable.

I recycle all year long and like to keep track of the amount I collect. In 2023, I made over $300 and am on track to do the same in 2024. Thank you E.W.P. for your beverage cans and bottles.

If you see empty aluminum beverage cans, plastic, glass water bottles, and soda bottles scattered about, know you are looking at easy money. Pick that up, head to the recycling center, and get paid immediately. Then, pat yourself on the back for doing a public service by removing litter and beautifying your community. Unfortunately, not all states offer this recycling program.

Busking—Are you skilled in singing, dancing, juggling, etc.? Share your entertainment skills with the world. Many will show appreciation with cash tips. I know of artists first discovered while performing on the streets: Robin Williams, Tiffany, Rod Stewart, Tracy Chapman, Justin Beeber, Ed Sheeran, and Benjamin Clementine. A couple of days ago, a woman was playing lovely music with her violin in the parking lot of our local grocery store. I and others gave her cash for her efforts.

High-Yield, Online Savings and Investment Accounts - Open an online savings account and set up an automatic deposit from your bank account into this savings account. The high-yield bank will pay you interest on that deposit. This means you are making money from your savings account balance every single day. It's an income stream. I am sharing a screenshot of my online savings account dashboard with Alliant Credit Union.

YTD Interest is money made while you sleep!

Financial expert Suze Orman recommends the following account program. I deposit at least $100 into the account each month. Alliant Credit Union will give you $100 after you have deposited $100 into a savings account with them for 12 consecutive months. After one year, you will have $1300 in your account, plus the interest. That is an 8.33% return on your money. This opportunity is still valid as of December 2024. Note: I am not compensated by Alliant Credit Union nor Suze Orman for sharing this information. Neither has endorsed this book or are connected to it in any way.

Saving your money and investing your money is an easy way to make money, all day long everyday, even while you are sleeping.

Donate Plasma—If you are over 18, you can make $30-$70 per donation, depending on where you live. There are health requirements and other criteria. You can donate twice weekly. You can also make additional money by referring others. It is reported to take two hours the first and second time. Once you are an established donor, it only takes an hour each time to donate, and you are compensated when you finish, per my sister.

Sell Your Hair—Yes, it's a thing. I remember one weird incident regarding this very matter. A few years ago, I was at a mall when a woman asked shoppers if they would like to sell their hair for $100 cash. I did not see her cut anyone's hair and pay them while there, but I learned that you can legitimately sell your hair for good money. I later searched the internet and found numerous companies that would buy human hair.

Per wikiHow, you could make $300 to $1000 for your hair. Pricing depends on how healthy it is, how long it is, and on its unique color and texture. A minimum of 10 inches is required for some companies and a minimum of 12 inches for others. It must not be dyed or treated. You must not smoke or drink alcohol. They only want healthy hair. Some buyers will take treated and/or dyed hair, but, again, it must be very well taken care of and healthy based on their standards. Surprise payday indeed.

That lady worked a sound side hustle to earn quick and easy money if someone took her offer. Also, that brave, head-full, healthy, long-haired person would make instant, easy money without spending any money. Realistically, though, it's a rare and unique money-making opportunity only if you are in the right place at the right time.

I am proud to brag that instead of selling her hair, my niece donated it to Locks of Love, an organization that makes custom hair pieces for children.

There you have it. Eight easy treasure hacks and one weird opportunity to swiftly get cash in hand without costing you a dime.

CHAPTER 3

LET'S MAKE MONEY

It's never too early to teach children about working, getting paid and managing their own money. Talking with kids about money should be normal.

For young kids under 13 years old, there is easy and quick money to earn daily. These are commonly called odd jobs. Many jobs can take an hour or less if they are brief assignments. I describe the job based on established relationships between family members, friends, and neighbors. Trust, skill levels, and maturity warrant scrutiny for these enterprising youngsters. Odd jobs are tried and true, relatively quick, and easy moneymakers for teenagers.

Formal, part-time jobs in retail and restaurants are additional possibilities for teens to earn income. One must take great care to balance any formal job with their school schedule and extracurricular activities. Also, federal and state laws are attached to employers, and limitations are based on age and work hours.

Getting paid for household chores or yard work is a great option. Growing up, this was also known as an 'allowance.' You might get paid that day, at the end of the week, or even longer. It depends on your family dynamic. A few friends got an allowance and never had to do chores. Talk about quick and easy money. The young entrepreneur, pictured below, made about $30 selling his old toys and grape juice at his grandparent's annual yard sale.

My 5-Year-Old Entrepreneur

Money-making options:

5 to 7-year-olds:

    1. Household chores and yard work to earn an allowance

    2. Going to work with Mom or Dad and getting paid

8 to 10-year-olds:

    1. Household chores and yard work to earn an allowance

    2. Going to work with Mom or Dad and getting paid

    3. Pet sitting/dog walking/poop scooping (with supervision)

11 & 12-year-olds:

    1. Household chores and yard work to earn an allowance

    2. Going to work with Mom or Dad and getting paid

    3. Pet sitting/dog walking/poop scooping (with supervision)

    4. Brief babysitting jobs (familial)

    5. Mowing lawns (with supervision)

    6. Car Washing (with supervision)

    7. Tutoring

When I was 12, a neighbor paid me one dollar to watch her baby for about 20-30 minutes while she showered. This continued for a few years until he was old enough to entertain himself for those minutes. Yep, easy money.

Below are a few money-making ideas for teenagers, young adults, and up:

13-year-olds:

    1. All the above listed jobs in this chapter

Below you will find a list of 10 jobs your teen can do, from home **online**. These website opportunities have a minimum age requirement of 13-years-old:

1. Mistplay.com: Earn gift cards by playing video games

2. Swagbucks.com: Complete surveys, watch videos and do other small tasks to earn rewards

3. SurveyJunkie.com: Complete surveys for cash or gift cards

4. Tutor.com: Provide online tutoring and get paid in cash

5. Fiverr.com: Offer your services in writing, graphic design, video editing or social media management

This is not a complete list, but these are the most popular and suitable teen sites. These sites offer appropriate opportunities for teens. Teens must check with a parent and/or guardian before signing up on these sites. You must set up a PayPal account to get paid, so a parent or guardian must help with this process.

Anyone can make money online.

Adults 18 and up:

1. All the above-listed jobs in this chapter

Numerous legitimate websites also offer ways to profit from a specific skill and fuel your interests. This is known as "freelancing," and you would be a "freelancer." These side hustles offer payouts the same day for small, quick assignments. These jobs are online and one can work from home with internet service.

1. **Freelance Writing**: You can write articles or blog posts for websites and blogs

2. **Online Assistant**: Help businesses with tasks like email management or scheduling

3. **Product Testing**: Test products and provide feedback to companies

4. **Website Testing**: Test websites for usability and get paid for your feedback

5. **Video Game Testing**: Test new games and report bugs or issues

It is essential to do your research and find reputable websites. Check the Better Business Bureau for status, do an internet search, read the company "about" tab, and look for site reviews in which you are interested. Read through the reviews to get a feel for the experiences of other freelancers. Know that longer and more detailed assignments may require more than one day to finish. Therefore, you must complete the job before getting paid.

The first part of this chapter offers problem-solving solutions for parents and guardians who want to limit their children's time on their devices. The online jobs for your teens are flexible and can be done from home, making them perfect for anyone looking to earn some extra cash.

Chapter 4

HIDDEN SPENDING

Forbes estimates the average US household spends over $552 monthly on streaming platforms and software service subscriptions. However, 45% of consumers forget to cancel their subscriptions after a free trial for services they do not use.

Consumers also tend to underestimate their monthly spending. One study showed that customers estimated their monthly subscriptions to be $86 when they were $219.

Simply checking your credit card charges for streaming subscription services keeps you aware of the costs associated with this type of spending. Cancel those subscriptions with minimal or no use. Did a streaming platform raise their rates? Call them and ask them to cancel your subscription. They will do everything they can to keep you as a customer, even lowering the rate to the previous charges, usually for a defined period. DirectTV made me this offer when their rate hit my maximum budget limit. I still chose to cancel their services and never missed them.

Canceling unused services or getting a better rate benefits you financially. It costs you nothing but time.

CREDIT CARD REWARDS

While examining your credit card account activities, ensure you take advantage of the reward benefits if you have that card. Redeem those cash rewards benefits directly into your checking account or put the funds toward the credit card balance. Redeem travel credits or airline miles for your next adventure. This can be done in minutes, again to your benefit.

UNCLAIMED PROPERTY SEARCH

I live in California and search the State Controller's Office (SCO) website each January to see if I or someone I know has unclaimed property.

This property ends up with the controller's office when various institutions cannot find the owners of their inactive accounts. Those assets, known as unclaimed property, are required by law to be turned over to the state after three years. Common types of unclaimed property include:

- Bank accounts
- Safe deposit box contents
- Stocks and bonds
- Mutual funds and dividends
- Certificates of Deposit
- Uncashed cashier's checks and money orders
- Insurance benefits

- Wages
- Estates
- Trust funds and escrow accounts
- Mineral interests and royalty payments
- Utility company refunds

These assets are turned over to the SCO when businesses cannot contact the property owners. The SCO holds these assets for as long as it takes the rightful owners or their heirs to claim them.

Searching and finding that you have unclaimed assets is quick and easy. There is no charge to search the database and file a claim. However, filing the claim and releasing the assets can take time.

COOL SERIAL NUMBERS

There are collectors who will pay you for U.S. currency with specific and uncommon serial numbers. I found this interesting internet site a few years ago.

This 1928 $10 Federal Reserve Note was listed for sale on the website for $2500.

CoolSerialNumbers.com is a website dedicated to collecting unique serial numbers on USA banknotes. The serial numbers are a distinctive sequence of numbers on the currency that can make a bill valuable to those who collect them. The site will buy, sell, and trade these bills. They also provide appraisal valuation services. The condition of the money will affect its appraised value.

Have fun simply inspecting your currency for a distinct pattern of serial numbers. You may find yourself flush with extra cash.

Chapter 5

WORK FROM HOME

Sell your stuff – Get rid of your unwanted, unused but still-useful things. You will declutter your home and not fill your local landfill with permanent waste.

Online – There is a platform for everything you may want to sell. I've used Facebook MarketPlace to sell and made purchases from Craigslist and eBay. I've seen things for sale on NextDoor and there are many other sites as well. If you have high end or specialty items, you can get top dollar on specialty sites like Poshmark for clothing and DeCluttr for electronics.

Yard sale – These sales are great because people love a good bargain, and some get serious about searching for treasures. They will come by early, and you can earn cash when you open for business. Get the kids involved and let them sell their things, too. My sister and brother-in-law are yard sale experts and have made hundreds of dollars in one day.

Sewing – Hemming, altering, and fixing zippers are in high demand on social media. So, monetize your skill set and work from home. Put up a sign in the yard and place posters on bulletin boards around town. Do good work, and word-of-mouth will keep the customers coming. My husband paid a woman in our neighborhood $40 to hem four pairs of slacks. It took her only 30 minutes. He got her name from comments in the NextDoor app.

Sell your extra fruit and vegetables – I have many neighbors who have vegetable gardens. They sell their extra produce from their driveways. A neighbor who lives close by sells her excess produce this way. There is something joyful about buying fruit and veggies right next to the rows where they were grown. I found her because she cleverly put a sign on the main road directing you to her little stand. Home-grown, seasonal produce is the best.

Neighborly Produce Stand - Make Money from your driveway.

Make Money with Your Pool - I know one neighbor who teaches swimming lessons in her pool. Another has adult water aerobics classes. You can get paid as soon as the class ends. One hot summer, my neighbor asked if she and her kids could swim in my pool. She did offer to pay, which I had not thought of, and humbly declined the cash. But, we had a blast that afternoon. It would be a nice, refreshing way to earn easy money in one day.

Notary – I have used notaries in office buildings and banks. This service was part of their regular employment. Some notaries take this specialty certification one step further and work from home. Two neighbors have signs advertising their services at the end of their driveways.

Sell Firewood - According to Home Advisor, a cord of wood sells for $125-$650, depending on the type and whether the customer picks it up or delivers it. If you have trees or access to cut trees., this might be your thing. My neighbor scans social media for free firewood, then gets it and sells it from his yard for customer pickup. He declares it's free and easy money, so I am sharing.

Chapter 6

CASH GIGS & SIDE HUSTLES 101

WHAT ARE THEY? I have read some articles and heard in a few social media videos that cash gigs and side hustles are being interchanged. Even in my research, internet search results would return the gig and side hustle labels for the same job. I made these distinctions that I believe define the two terms as follows:

Cash Gig:

- **Short-Term**: Often one-time or occasional tasks

- **Quick Pay**: Typically pays out immediately or within a very short period

- **Fair Pay**: Typically lower than a side hustle

- **Flexibility**: Can be done quickly, often on the same day

- **Employment Law and Tax Risks**: Done without reporting to authorities

Cash gigs are also known as "under the table" side jobs, these refer to work that's done informally without official documentation or reporting to tax authorities in some cases.

Common examples of cash gigs:

- **Babysitting**: Caring for children you know

- **Yard Work**: Mowing lawns, gardening or other yard maintenance

- **Handyperson Services**: Performing minor home repairs or maintenance

- **Cleaning Services**: Providing cleaning for homes and or offices

- **Tutoring**: Offering education help outside of a formal school setting

- **Pet Services**: Pet sitting, pet walking and poop scooping for pet owners

- **Musician**: Get paid cash to perform solo or as part of a band

- **Moving Services**: Help people transport their belongings when they move

- **Senior Transport**: Offer transportation to senior citizens for appointments and errands

- **Pet Transport**: Offer to transport pets for appointments or travel

- **Laundry Collection and Delivery**: Delivery to and from home and or the office

- **Junk Hauling**: Collect and haul junk from homes and business parking lots

- **Sidewalk Artist**: Paint, draw, sketch and make balloon animals at events for tips

- **Wedding Services**: Photograph or video weddings

Side Hustle:

- **Ongoing Commitment:** Often a more consistent effort alongside primary employment & offers flexibility and is tailored for your interests and skills

- **Varied Pay**: Has a few quick pay options and regular or irregular income depending on the nature of the hustle

- **Builds Over Time:** Can evolve into a larger income stream or even a full-time business

- **Employment and Tax Documentation**: Companies are obligate to report earnings to authorities

Here are some common examples of legitimate side hustles:

- **Freelance Writing**: Creating content for blogs, websites and businesses

- **Graphic Design**: Designing logos, flyers, book covers and social media graphics

- **Online Tutoring**: Teaching subjects in which you are proficient

- **Virtual Assistant**: Offering remote administrative support

- **Etsy Shop**: Sell handmade crafts, vintage items or digital products

- **Drop Shipping**: Running an online store without stored inventory

- **Social Media Management**: Managing social medica accounts for businesses or influencers

- **Affiliate Marketing**: Promoting products or services and earning a commission on those sales

- **Photography**: Selling photos on stock photo website or offering photography services

- **Blogging/Vlogging**: Creating content on a blog or video channel (like YouTube) and making money via ads, sponsorships or merchandise

- **Crafts**: Selling your craft creations at local markets or online

- **House and or Pet Sitting/Walking**: Caring for homes and or pets while owners are away

- **Fitness Coaching**: Offering online fitness sessions and personalized training

- **Podcasting**: Starting a podcast and making money via ads and sponsorships

- **Website Flipping**: Buying and selling websites

A cash gig is a quick and short-term way to earn money, often paid out on the same day, while a side hustle is more of an ongoing effort that can build into primary employment over time with a significant income possible.

Chapter 7

ONLINE QUICK CASH GIGS

NUMEROUS GIG WEBSITES WILL pay you to play video games, complete surveys, shop online, watch ads, watch movies, listen to music, download and test apps, pay for your search history, enter contests, and so on. These gigs are popular with users who want to earn money without much effort.

To earn easy money with same-day payouts, the amount per gig is lower than that for sites with higher pay per gig. My research notes a range of 25 cents to five dollars to complete some tasks for the sites listed below. Higher-paying gigs do not pay out quickly and require more of an undertaking. Those gigs are not included in this book.

Sign-up is easy on the following list of sites. You will need a PayPal account. When you have finished signing up, you can start earning immediately. Choose your interests and go for it. You get paid cash into your PayPal account or gift cards to your favorite businesses. You must earn the minimum amount set forth by the site before payout. You get to choose how you get paid. This book does not include sites that only pay in gift cards or by check. I have listed sites with a minimum payout of $5 in earnings or less.

As of 2024, the following are popular gigs with reportedly easy and quick ways to get cash payouts the same day, and they are all free to start:

Available in a Limited Countries:

BrandedSurveys: Complete surveys. (US, Canada and UK only)

SurveyJunkie: Complete surveys. (US, Canada and Australia only)

Scrambly: Mobile Games, Complete Offers (US and Canada Only)

InboxDollars: Surveys, Shopping offers, Play Games and more. (US only)

HeyPiggy: Surveys (US, Canada, UK, Germany, France and a few other countries)

QuickRewards: Surveys, Watching Ads, Playing Games, etc (US and Canada only)

EARN EASY MONEY IN ONE DAY

ONLINE QUICK CASH GIGS

Available in Numerous Countries:

Swagbucks.com :Surveys, Mobile Games, Shopping, Trivia, Watching Ads, (Global)

Freecash.com/en: Cash surveys, play games, watch videos, installing apps, etc (Global)

Attapoll.com: Complete Surveys. (Global)

PrimeOpinions.com: Surveys (Global)

Ipsosisay.com/en-us: Surveys (Available in over 100 countries)

Toluna.com: Surveys, Polls, Entering Contests (Available in over 60 Countries)

There is always a question of the legitimacy of any website that claims one can make easy and quick money. I found a few good articles and blogs about the sites I have listed above. They have been well-tested and included user reviews. Please refer to the resources section of this book for further reading if you like.

User reviews of the websites with the most significant payouts generated the most scam-type claims. Some payout minimums start at $25. Earning those minimum amounts could take a long time, leading users to believe they were scammed.

There were also complaints of being "kicked off" sites and losing all they had earned up to that point. Per the articles, users may not have realized they had violated site rules. The main rule is that you may not use a VPN when accessing their site. It is important to read and understand all the rules and requirements.

Chapter 8

LEGITIMATE SIDE HUSTLES

For semi-skilled and skilled gig workers, side hustles are a popular way to pursue your passion and interests. You will benefit by perfecting your skills and padding your income. This additional source of earnings could lead to a full-time career.

After extensive research and one testimonial, I have listed below the legitimate side hustles that will pay out immediately or within one day of the delivery or assignment completion. They are also free to start.

Home-based/Online:

1. **Freelance Writing**: FlexJobs and ProBlogger offer same-day payouts upon completion for quick assignments

2. **Graphic Design**: Similar to freelance writing, quick design jobs have same-day payouts on Fiverr or UpWork

3. **Online Tutoring**: Cambly and OutSchool offer same day payouts, but check the payment policies for requirements

4. **Virtual Assistant**: Depending on the client and the nature of the tasks, you will get paid the same day on Freelancer, Fiverr and Upwork

Vehicle Required:

1. **Ridesharing**: Platforms like Uber and Lyft offer instant cash-out options.

2. **Food Delivery**: Services like Uber Eats, DoorDash, and Grubhub often provide same-day payouts.

3. **Advertising**: Get paid to wrap your car with advertisements through services like Wrapify or Carvertise.

The opportunities are endless for anyone wanting to boost income with a good side hustle.

My cousin drives for DoorDash. She works full-time for a traditional company and has a cleaning business side hustle. DoorDash deliveries earn her easy and speedy money when she needs it.

Chapter 9

SCAM AND TAX IMPLICATIONS

There are scam websites explicitly designed to separate you from your money and your work product and/or steal your identity. We should all recognize the signs of scams by now and be able to avoid them. However, scammers are very good at what they do. I have seen many knowledgeable but unsuspecting people get scammed in various ploys. Do not let a scam be a part of your story. Please avoid the following:

DO NOT pay fees to sign up for gig and side hustle websites. There is no job there, and they may take your money. You will never hear from them again.

DO NOT give out your personal identification information. Again, there is no job there, and you may become a victim of identity theft and fraud.

DO NOT accept payment first before you've done any work. The scam works by you depositing a check or money order into your personal bank account. The scammer will then relate they have paid you too much and ask for some of the money back. You send them money back. Then, your bank informs you that the check or money order is fraudulent. You are now out of the money you sent and all the bank fees associated with a bad check or money order.

DO NOT accept freelance work assignments during an interview or orientation. You might be asked to complete a job as part of the hiring process, with no discussion about pay or contract regarding payment. They may want your work product without paying you. You should already have a portfolio of work products showcasing your skills. Offer a sample from your portfolio. If they insist you accept their request, walk away. There is no job here.

INCOME TAXES

When you get paid money to work, you are earning income. In the United States of America, it is the law that you must pay income taxes. There are a few exceptions.

PLEASE PAY YOUR TAXES.

There is free software to help you file, or you can hire a professional if necessary. The Internal Revenue Service (IRS) has penalties and consequences that can be negatively life-altering for failure to do so.

Chapter 10

CONCLUSION

MAKING EASY MONEY FROM my book is a valuable way for anyone to boost their income, even if only a little at a time. I have highlighted quick income tips and tricks. I truly enjoy recycling for the satisfaction knowing I am taking care of my neighborhood, my community and mother earth.

Please join me, whether working through the treasure hacks noted in the first chapter or making better income from any online gig and side hustle suggestions, you can make the most of your spare time by being creative using these simple strategies.

CONCLUSION

EARN EASY MONEY IN ONE DAY

You have a good start to get quick cash and boost your income. Pass on your new found knowledge and show other readers where they can find the same inspiration.

Simply by leaving your honest opinion of this book on Amazon, you'll show other readers where they can find the information they're looking for. They can be amused and learn to make easy money in one day too.

The topic of making money is on our minds and it can truly help when we pass on our knowledge – and you can assist me in doing just that. Thank you for your help.

>>>> Please use the link below to leave your review on Amazon:

Amazon Review: EARN EASY MONEY IN ONE DAY

>>>> Or hover your cell phone camera over the QR-code image below, tap the yellow button that appears to leave an Amazon review:

Amazon Review

Chapter 11

RESOURCES

Blake, T. (2024a, May 24). *10 legit survey apps that pay instantly*. WebMonkey. Retrieved December 6, 2024, from https://www.webmonkey.com/survey-apps-that-pay-instantly/

Blake, T. (2024, September 3). *2024 Side Hustle Database*. Web Monkey. Retrieved December 6, 2024, from https://www.webmonkey.com/side-hustle-database/

Blake, T. (2024b, November 14). *Is Scrambly Legit? – My 2024 Review & Earnings Proof*. WebMonkey. Retrieved December 6, 2024, from https://www.webmonkey.com/is-scrambly-io-legit/

Orentas, G. (2024, June 13). Streaming trends for 2024: 44% report streaming costs increasing over the last year. *Forbes Home*. https://www.forbes.com/home-improvement/internet/streaming-survey/#:~:text=People%20are%20spending%20an%20average%20of%20$46%20per%20month%20on,cancel%20and%20subsequently%20incurring%20charges.

Greenlight Team (Ed.). (2024, October 31). *19 Online Jobs for Teens and Students to Work From Home*. Greenlight. Retrieved December 6, 2024, from https://greenlight.com/learning-center/earning/online-jobs-for-teens

Grossman, A. (2024, November 1). *34+ Online Jobs for Teenagers that Pay (Jobs for Ages 13 and Up)*. Money Prodigy. Retrieved December 6, 2024, from https://www.moneyprodigy.com/online-jobs-for-teenagers-that-pay/

Madison, B. (2024, February 16). *How Much Do You Get Paid to Donate Plasma?* GoodRx. Retrieved December 6, 2024, from https://www.goodrx.com/health-topic/finance/how-much-donating-plasma-pays

California State Controller's Office. (2024). *Search for Unclaimed Property*. Retrieved December 7, 2024, from

U.S. Department Of Labor. (2024, June 13). *Selected State Child Labor Standards Affecting Minors Under 18 in Non-farm Employment as of June 13, 2024*. U.S. Department of Labor Wage And Hour Division. Retrieved December 6, 2024, from

wikiHow. (2024, June 25). *How to Sell Your Hair*. Retrieved December 6, 2024, from https://www.sco.ca.gov/search_upd.html

7 Same-Day pay Jobs (And other ways to get paid instantly). (2024, May 6). sidehustles.com. Retrieved December 6, 2024, from https://sidehustles.com/same-day-pay-jobs/

15 Side Hustles That Pay Daily in 2024: Get Paid Today. (2024, June 14). Skillademia. Retrieved December 6, 2024, from https://www.skillademia.com/blog/side-hustles-that-pay-daily/

Andre, M. (2024, June 27). *11 Easy Online Jobs for Teens (13-18 Years Old)*. The Ways to Wealth. Retrieved December 6, 2024, from https://www.thewaystowealth.com/online-jobs-for-teens/

Online Jobs for Teens. (2023, October 16). CreditDonkey. Retrieved December 6, 2024, from https://www.creditdonkey.com/online-jobs-teens.html

The Income Informer. (2024). *17 Best Side Hustles That Pay Daily: Get Paid for Work from Home Jobs!* Retrieved December 6, 2024, from https://theincomeinformer.com/side-hustles-that-pay-daily/#google_vignette

Campbell, H. (2024, February 9). *Tax Guide for Uber & Lyft Drivers (Updated for 2024).* Ride Share Guy. Retrieved December 6, 2024, from https://therideshareguy.com/rideshare-taxes/

Hoyt, B. (2024, January 2). *DoorDash Taxes Made Easy (2024 Tax Guide).* M$M. Retrieved December 6, 2024, from https://millennialmoneyman.com/doordash-taxes/

Earnings From Survey Sites Are Taxable Income. (2023, March 6). The Penny Hoarder. Retrieved December 6, 2024, from https://www.thepennyhoarder.com/taxes/survey-sites-and-taxes/

Johnson, D. (2019, July 6). *8 side hustles that are actually scams.* Business Insider. Retrieved December 7, 2024, from https://www.businessinsider.com/8-side-hustles-that-are-actually-scams-2019-7

www.ingramcontent.com/pod-product-compliance
Lightning Source LLC
Chambersburg PA
CBHW070942220526
45469CB00007B/2481